47 Little Love Boosters for a Happy Marriage

CONNECT AND INSTANTLY DEEPEN YOUR BOND NO MATTER HOW BUSY YOU ARE

By Marko Petkovic

Contents

Foreword

WHETHER YOUR RELATIONSHIP is a new romance or one that has passed the test of time, there might be days when you wonder how to keep the fire burning.

This book is about simple things that you can do to reconnect and stay connected with your partner no matter what stage - or state - your relationship is in right now. It is about the little things that you can do to keep the fire burning and feel alive *every day*, no matter how busy you are.

Life happens, career happens, kids happen, and the mortgage happens. As time passes and you settle into a comfortable relationship, you may find it all too easy to relax and forget to reconnect with your partner in meaningful ways.

Before you know it you can be more like business partners who happen to be raising children, managing the housework, and paying the mortgage together. Suddenly, you're more like roommates when you were once madly in love.

Most people think this is what happens to couples after a while. We think it's supposed to be like this, that it's "normal". So many of us choose to

1

accept this as a fact of life, a law of nature. We set our lives on cruise control, thinking our marriage will take care of itself. Because all you need is love, right? After all, it's what the Beatles sang!

Well, that's just plain wrong.

Sure, successful couples love each other deeply, but they don't rely on loving feelings to come naturally. They create them. Moreover, they create them consistently, every day.

Just letting life go on, and not doing anything about the gaps in your life is not going to be enough. Love is an act of doing, not having.

Still, after a long day at work it may be difficult to think of doing something meaningful for your spouse when you know you have to take care of the kids first. Drive them to skating, piano, or soccer, pick them up, make dinner, take care of the housework and finish dozens of other little things on the list. Answer emails from work, do a load of laundry, and pack the lunches for tomorrow. It takes a toll.

It drains your energy out and at times it can be overwhelming. Then if you're lucky enough to be finally able to collapse onto your couch to catch your breath, you're simply too tired for anything else. Deep inside, you feel empty. Something is missing. Another day has passed.

It happens to many of us and it's not your fault.

This is one of the main reasons why couples who love each other deeply slowly but surely start losing their connection: that bond they once shared. Gradually, they end up spending most of their time together fulfilling these everyday, more demanding aspects of their relationship, while forgetting to reconnect on a daily basis. In other words, they're *forgetting* to enjoy the thousands of tiny little pleasurable aspects of being together.

If this sounds like you, you've come to a good place. Because with the help of this book you'll have a choice. This book is about simple things you can do to connect and instantly create a deeper bond with your partner in spite of your busy schedule.

Perhaps your spouse or partner has complained they're missing "the old days"? Maybe it is you who noticed the change and perhaps it is you who feel you're drifting apart? Maybe you miss that warmth and the bond you once had. Do you want it back?

I know exactly how you feel. It happened to me.

Three years ago my dear wife and I were struggling in our marriage. When I say struggling I mean we came to point when my wife suggested a divorce.

Looking back, our marriage started to go downhill just after our second son was born, and I left the corporate world to start my own company. This was the year when we actually had two babies: our son and a new company. To get the company going over the course of the next few years I did very little other than work. As a result the company flourished and I felt successful. Not surprisingly, things at home started to falter.

The scary part is that drifting apart and getting disconnected wasn't an event we could clearly point the finger to. In our case it took years. Even then, when we finally became aware that we were not so close anymore it was still emotionally "easier" to dismiss the early signs of our relationship getting weaker. It was "easier" to pretend we were fine, even though we could hardly remember the last time we did a nice thing for each other . . . just because. It was simpler to think "we're fine, this happens to most couples" when we couldn't remember when was the last time we were "just us", like in the old days.

Deep inside though, we knew it wasn't supposed to be like that. It certainly wasn't what we wanted. Ultimately, after many years of expecting things to get better we had built so many walls around our hearts that my wife proposed a divorce.

We almost lost hope.

Thankfully we scraped and dug our way out without any professional counseling. We found a way to crumble those walls between us and rediscover that connection we once had (and still have) and our marriage is now something we hold precious, and protect.

Inspired by our success, I wrote Amazon bestsellers the *Feel Good Marriage* and my most recent book *The 5 Little Love Rituals* (more information at the back of this book).

Looking back it feels almost embarrassing how simple things can be, though. With just a pinch of common sense, some knowledge, and a dash of loving and caring discipline, things can be simple.

I believe keeping things simple is a good thing. People are more likely to start doing and keep on doing things in life that are simple. We're all more likely to have success that way.

This book is about those simple things. The nice little things in life that cost no money and require little to no time but matter the most. Moreover, they require no cooperation from your spouse. It's completely within your control and you can start right now.

The results are magical.

How to Use This Book

EVEN THOUGH THIS is a paper book, it is intentionally designed to be interactive. That's because my goal is to help you not just read this book but actually use it to your advantage.

For this reason, you will find "signposts" along the way in this book that will lead you to an online bonus section.

The bonus section contains PDF cheat sheets designed to help you start getting positive results even more quickly. By downloading them to your phone you'll have inspiration at your fingertips even when you're temporarily out of ideas and you don't have this book handy.

The bonus section comes with a full-length audiobook too. You can listen to it while driving the car, cleaning the house, working out, or going for a jog—when your mind is available. This way you don't have to take any extra time out of your life to make the happy marriage you and your partner deserve.

When you register for the first time you will receive your private permanent link to your members area with all the cheat sheets from the signposts you will come to as you read. And, you'll also be eligible to receive the goodies that I occasionally send only to my VIP readers.

If you're curious to get a sneak peek at the bonus section right now, visit:

http://geni.us/47bonuses

Alternatively, you can scan the QR code below with your phone.

CHAPTER 1

The Icing on the Cake

*"You will never change your life
until you change something you do daily.
The secret of your success
is found in your daily routine."*

— *John C. Maxwell*

MOST PEOPLE WOULD AGREE that anyone who wants to lose weight but only diets twice a year, or walks around the block once per month, can't expect to have their body in perfect shape, right?

Isn't it then interesting that when it comes to their own relationship most people expect exactly that? They believe that you must pull off something big and extravagant so that your efforts will matter and will be noticed.

While it's wonderful to be able to enjoy a nice gift for your birthday and a fancy dinner once in a while, it's a dangerous illusion to think that's all you need.

That alone isn't enough though. It's more like the icing on the cake.

What you want is a relationship that's sustainable, not some hyped-up joy, or a temporary rush in loving feelings that comes because you've just had a week without the kids, and read a couple of good books on a remote beach under the tropical sun (although that wouldn't hurt once in a while).

How can you do that?

How can you bake the cake first and only then start thinking of putting the icing on top as well?

The answer has two sides.

The first one lies in the pioneering research of Dr. John Gottman, one of the few living legends in marital therapy. Over a number of years he conducted a series of interviews and recordings with hundreds of couples, and found interesting commonality among successful couples.

Research showed that couples who've stayed together have five times more positive interactions than negative ones.

I can only confirm this from my personal experience.

When my wife and I were at the peak of our problems it was exactly this treasure chest of good memories (positive interactions) from the early days that helped save our butts. It gave us strength to push through the stormy times, try new things and finally start crumbling the walls around our hearts that we've built over the years.

Think of it like making small deposits of money to your savings account every day. The same goes for your relationship only in this case it's your emotional account. We call it *The Love Account*. When it comes to this Love Account, positive interactions are deposits. We'll talk more about those in just a minute. Withdrawals, on the other hand, are made up of negative interactions, for example disagreements and fights, or anything requiring an apology. Both types of interactions are normal, and both happen every day.

Your job is to make the number of positive interactions outnumber the negative ones by far.

Now you know why big gestures will never do the trick, no matter how pleasant they might be. They are simply not frequent enough. They could never be frequent enough.

There's only one Valentines' day in a year, and one day when it's your loved one's birthday. There's just one day when you celebrate your wedding anniversary, right? And, unless you're Sir Richard Branson, you can't just hop on a plane and whisk your loved one away to a tropical island every week, right?

But that's okay. That's why those things are just the icing on the cake.

So what's the cake then? How do we get it?

We're looking for something sustainable that is going to repeatedly produce positive interactions in your relationship. Every day, week, month and year. Notice the key word *repeatedly*. That's the other side of the answer. Our brain loves repetition because it's how we learn and how we memorize things. Therefore, what we're really looking for is a system, a set of *love habits* that will consistently create loving thoughts, heartfelt affection, and feelings of connection. Personally I prefer using the term *Love Rituals*, and here's why.

Love rituals are more than habits.
They are the repetition of deliberate acts for our loved ones through which we show respect and affection. Love rituals are special, because your relationship is special.

Love rituals should not be put in the same basket as other more mundane habits that we develop in life, like brushing your teeth in the morning. These are much more important and much more special.

Additionally, the term ritual implies a kind of secrecy. Rightly so, because to other couples who haven't yet figured it out, it looks almost like magic. They ask, "How can you still be so connected after so many years?"

Something else becomes obvious too.

We're looking for *simple* things. If any kind of love ritual is ever going to stick it should be simple so it can be implemented and memorized easily.

This makes it much easier to pick the most promising love rituals that fit the criteria.

We call them The 5 Little Love Rituals.

CHAPTER 2

The 5 Little Love Rituals

"Sow a thought,
and you reap an act;
Sow an act,
and you reap a habit;
Sow a habit,
and you reap a character;
Sow a character,
and you reap a destiny."

— Samuel Smiles

WHEN MY *FEEL GOOD MARRIAGE* book was released, I received many emails from my dear readers telling me that the book helped them the most by inspiring them to develop new habits for their relationships. I can't tell you how happy I was to hear that.

It also made me curious.

What if I could go back and distill just a couple of the most important simple-to-implement habits that successful couples use to keep recreating loving feelings for each other every day—in spite of their busy lives?

What if I could identify the "best performing" love rituals, the ones that bring *the best results for the least effort?*

By going back to my old notes, and talking to successful couples from my coaching practice about what they did right and wrong in their relationships, I was able to identify *five little love rituals* successful couples do that fit the above-mentioned criteria. I call them "little" because they take very little of your time, and yet they mean so much.

Each of the five little love rituals touches one vital aspect of couples' connection and makes their bond stronger every time they use it. In short, the *five little love rituals* provide a simple way to:

- Make your spouse's day and make them instantly happy. The beauty is, while making your partner happy, you yourself are becoming happier too (Love Ritual #1).
- Keep up with your partner's life and prevent ending up living with a stranger some day (Love Ritual #2).
- Be physically intimate even without having sex (Love Ritual #3).
- Spend meaningful time together even if your schedule is jam-packed and your days are exhausting (Love Ritual #4).

- Feel excitement again even after years of marriage, while at the same time preventing getting bored with each other (like so many couples eventually do). That's because as much as we crave closeness, stability, and predictability, we also feel a desire for novelty. This aspect is more powerful than you might have thought, because when done right it works like a natural aphrodisiac too (Love Ritual #5).

Still, let us walk before we run.

This book has one purpose, and one purpose only. While the above-mentioned five love rituals work amazingly well indeed, and I do strongly encourage you to start doing them when the time is right for you, with this book I wanted to shine a light on Love Ritual #1.

That's because it really is the lowest hanging fruit.

You can start doing it literally right now (or right when your spouse gets home). The best thing? It won't take you more than a couple of minutes of your time—sometimes only seconds!

So, without further delay, let's dive in and discover how you can start reconnecting with your spouse today!

CHAPTER 3

The Little Things That Matter the Most

"Life is made up,
not of great sacrifices or duties,
but of little things,
in which smiles and kindness,
and small obligations given habitually,
are what preserve the heart
and secure comfort."

– Humphry Davy

IN THIS CHAPTER we're going to talk about a very simple love ritual. Perhaps it is the simplicity of it that makes it so easy to overlook and dismiss, even though it's well within our grasp.

It's the ritual of doing nice little things for each other every day. We also call these nice little things the "love boosters" because:

- You don't need cooperation from your partner to start.
- They take very little of your time—sometimes only seconds!
- You can do them at home.
- Most of them are free.

It's simply amazing how those tiny tokens of appreciation can go such a long way. Sure, it's nice to get a birthday present, but do we really need all that stuff? Isn't it those little signs of appreciation from our partner that really make us feel loved?

Most couples eventually come to a stage in life when they start wondering where the spark went. Some people say they've grown apart. Others complain about how they always fight, and how angry they are at one another. Chances are they stopped doing the little things for each other a long time ago.

On the other hand, couples who are successful nourish their relationship regularly and often. They don't set their life on cruise control, expecting a happy life.

Here's what they do.

The Most Important Question

Successful couples ask themselves this simple question.

What can I do to make my partner's life more pleasurable TODAY?

Notice the word *today*. This is one of the most important and powerful questions you should ask yourself *every day*.

It's how you're showing up, how you're loving. It's how you're giving every day.

Nice thoughts said aloud, a gentle touch, a kind smile, or a sincere thank you are just a few examples of the little things that matter so much. Something as simple as "You make the best coffee," or "Thank you for walking the dog every night," smiling at each other as you pass in the hall, or simply holding hands.

Things you think about, but never say or do.

Do something nice and beautiful for your partner just because today you paused and thought about how lucky you are to have someone so special in your life.

Because you enjoy making your spouse feel good. Because you know it will make them feel loved. Just because.

Despite the fact that they are "little" they mean so much. What will impress your loved one the most will often be the little things. Your loved one will be touched that you took the time to show them that you care. Your thoughtful actions will be noticed.

What's better than that warm feeling in your heart when you realize your partner is thinking about you, and did something—just because?

Showing your partner that you care and that they are special to you does not need to be complicated. Some of the most touching ways of saying I LOVE YOU are the simplest and most appreciated.

If you're married or in a committed relationship you have already taken one of the most important decisions in life, if not *the* most important.

You're spending your life with another human being, whom you love and want to grow old with, and who has a huge impact on how successful you'll be in life.

Therefore, making your partner happy, making your spouse's life a bit more pleasurable repeatedly and consistently every day will accumulate over time and make a huge difference.

An Invitation to a Journey

At this point I'd like to extend a special invitation to you.

It is no secret that discovering new things (or things we have long forgotten) works best when it's a multi-sensory experience. Therefore, I invite you to take a little journey with me. Let's make the experience of discovering the *Love Boosters* even stronger.

I invite you to read the rest of this chapter by browsing through the *47 Little Love Boosters* with me. It will put you on the fast track to start getting loving inspiration and making new associations even quicker.

As we all know, to create permanent change, we must put forth continuing efforts—even if those efforts are simple and easy.

But you might not have this book with you when you most need an idea!

However, you probably have a phone where you can have a casual peek and attract no suspicion from your spouse.

That's why I went ahead and created a short, beautifully illustrated cheat sheet. It's called the *Golden Collection of 47 Little Love Boosters.*

It's a special PDF version of all the *love boosters* that you're going to get familiar with in just a moment.

It's waiting for you in the bonus member's area of this book and it was designed to be crystal-clear and readable on your smartphone or tablet.

So, it might be a good idea to download and save the *Golden Collection* right now. This way you can have a quick peek and get inspiration any time and anywhere you want.

Even if you don't have your smartphone or tablet handy right now, I still encourage you to activate the Golden Collection in the bonus section as soon as you can.

That's because you'll get a permanent link from me and you will be able to access it later.

http://geni.us/47bonuses

The 47 Little Love Boosters

In the same way that life is not predictable, the *Little Love Boosters* in the list below are put together in no particular order. They are a sample of ideas and suggestions as to how you can show your thoughtfulness and caring that cost no money and take just a tiny fraction of your time. Furthermore, they don't require cooperation from your partner. They are little things that you can start doing right now.

It may be tempting to scoff at some of them as "common sense". And you would be right. Too often though it's common sense that is not being applied to common practice.

If you can't remember when was the last time you did at least a couple of these ideas, now is the time to start. If on the other hand you are doing some of the love boosters already, you're still going to find something that'll get your imagination going.

Lastly, no one knows your spouse better than you do. Use the list below as your starting point and it will keep you going for quite a while. In the meantime, you'll start coming up with plenty of your own ideas and combinations.

Then watch magic start to happen.

Without further delay, let's start sending the love boosters to your loved one now!

1. Say "Thank you."

Love Booster 1: SAY "THANK YOU." DON'T TAKE YOUR LOVED ONE FOR GRANTED.

Even if it seems commonplace to you, when was the last time you said to your loved one "Thank you for a delicious meal today," or "Thank you for mowing the lawn today." Just do it and observe. You'll see the immediate reaction on your partner's face and that's invaluable. These two tiny little words have more power in them then you might have ever thought. Rightly so, because they show you're not taking the love of your life for granted. You're showing gratitude.

2. Greet with a hug, part with a kiss.

Give a loving look and a kiss to your love as soon as you walk in the door and just as you leave each day.

Love Booster 2   GREET WITH A HUG, PART WITH A KISS

It has been scientifically proven that being surrounded by loving people hugging them, kissing them, and smiling has a profound positive effect on babies' wellbeing. We're no different now as adults, except that we are now so busy and constantly in a hurry.

There's neuroscience behind this.

Remember this, skin is our biggest organ. There are approximately five million touch receptors in our skin, 3,000 in each fingertip alone. As such, hugging sets off a powerful response in our brains. It reduces stress and makes us feel good. In that sense, it's vital for getting the feelings of closeness that we all need so much.

Besides showing your affection, there's another reason to smile at your partner when you part and you see them again (or for that matter as frequently as possible).

Did you know that by smiling (even when you don't feel like it!), you can make yourself feel good for no reason at all? That's because the center of your brain that controls the facial muscles that make your smile happen is coincidentally (or not!) neighboring the very part of the brain that is also responsible for production of serotonin. Serotonin controls sleep, memory, learning, temperature and—you guessed it—mood and behavior.

There's a third reason, and this is the most important one. Your loved one's subconscious starts associating you with something pleasant every time they see you.

Now you tell me—is there any better way to start a day? Is there a more joyful way to come back home again?

By the way: if you're not doing this already, try the same principle on your kids and watch their response after a while.

3. Ask "What can I do for you today?"

When you're having your morning coffee, why not ask "What can I do for you today?" Sure, your spouse might be surprised at first. They might even have something to ask you, but may have been worried you wouldn't have time.

Love Booster 3 ASK "WHAT CAN I DO FOR YOU TODAY?"

This tiny little question (and follow-up) carries more thoughtfulness in itself than any gift that you can ever bring to your loved one.

4. Let your loved one know how proud you are of them.

Love Booster 4 LET YOUR LOVED ONE KNOW HOW PROUD YOU ARE OF THEM

Show enthusiasm for your partner's personal and work-related successes. Don't forget to celebrate their accomplishments! Let them see how happy you are for them!

"Little things seem nothing,
but they give peace,
like those meadow flowers
which individually seem odorless
but all together perfume the air."

- Georges Bernanos

5. Express admiration out loud.

Say openly how fabulous your loved one looks. Don't assume they know how you feel about them. When your partner dresses to go out, pay attention and admire them. Let your partner know when they're wearing a color that really compliments their eyes or hair.

6. Shine a light on your partner in public.

Go ahead and brag a little. Compliment you partner in public often.

If you're talking in a group and it's appropriate to the conversation say something like "Kate makes the most incredible roast" or "Mike mows the lawn like a Persian carpet" and give them a loving look while you're talking about them.

7. Bring breakfast to bed and eat together.

It might not be practical to do this every day (and it doesn't need to be), but why not wake up early and surprise your loved one with a crunchy hot toast and tea?

Do this on a weekend when you have some more time and watch your partner's face, especially if they are not used to such acts of kindness from you.

"You can give without loving,
but you can never love
without giving."

- Robert Louis Stevenson

8. Leave a steamy memento.

LEAVE A STEAMY MEMENTO

If you leave for work early, leave your spouse's favorite coffee on the table.

9. Kiss them unexpectedly.

KISS THEM UNEXPECTEDLY

Just how often do you kiss your loved one? Has the kiss turned into a move you two only do during foreplay? A kiss is a powerful connection. Kiss your spouse often, even if it's just a casual peck on the lips—especially if your children are looking.

Not only will you show your spouse your devotion and affection but your children will unconsciously pick up the very same behavior patterns from you and use them later in their adult life.

10. Say "I care" with nutritional flair.

Love Booster SAY "I CARE" WITH NUTRITIONAL FLAIR

Leave a glass of freshly squeezed orange juice on the counter to make sure your spouse starts the day with a vitamin boost.

11. Hug them for no reason.

In the same way as kissing your spouse unexpectedly, try hugging them for no particular reason.

It's an extremely simple yet powerful way to show your affection and add another small "deposit" to your love account. For the same reason as mentioned for the Love Booster #2, you'll feel better yourself too.

Touching and cuddling releases oxytocin, one of the "happy neurochemicals" that our brains produce.

You may not know this, but oxytocin is also released through eating fatty foods. Think about that the next time you finish that second bag of salty chips! Instead, you might just want to hug your loved one a little.

12. Let your partner sleep in.

On Saturday morning, wake up early. Take the kids out and leave your loved one to sleep later than usual.

If you want an extra loving look from your spouse, just before leaving house leave a juice plate of fresh fruit along with some croissants on the table and a loving note "Slept well? I love you!"

13. Send your spouse a loving email or text message in the middle of the day.

This one is self explanatory, right?

If you suspect or know your partner will have a particularly difficult day, send some words of love and encouragement.

It will be just seconds for you but it might mean a world to them. It will show you're thoughtful. Even after years, I still have some of the messages my wife sent me stored in my phone.

"It's the little details that are vital.
Little things make big things happen."

- John Wooden

14. Partner up! Do the chores together.

Offer to do the dishes or fold the clothes together. Use the time to talk about the day.

15. Show interest.

If you are a woman, remember that your husband might like to have you show an interest in what he is doing. What's under the hood of the car might not interest you, but giving your spouse a few moments to share his expertise will make him feel good. Take the time to listen, and let him know you appreciate his role and the work he does.

16. Unexpectedly drop by with a little something from across the street.

UNEXPECTEDLY DROP BY WITH A LITTLE SOMETHING FROM ACROSS THE STREET

If you want to be important in your loved one's life, the bakery is a good place to start. Drop by your spouse's office with a cupcake from the shop across the street on your lunch break.

17. Draw funny faces on the eggs in the refrigerator.

Okay, this one is outright silly. In any case, that's intentional. And powerful too!

Fun time, connecting with each other in laughter, releases endorphins in your brains–same as when you eat chocolate or have sex. Especially once we get comfortable in our relationship, it's all too easy to forget about this.

Love Booster 17 DRAW FUNNY FACES ON THE EGGS IN THE REFRIGERATOR

The last place you expect any kind of message is our refrigerator, right? Use that to your advantage! Add a little loving note if you will.

18. Wake up first and prepare your partner's favorite breakfast.

Love Booster 18 WAKE UP FIRST AND PREPARE YOUR PARTNER'S FAVORITE BREAKFAST

Plan to wake up first—before the kids even start getting out of bed. Silently prepare your partner's favorite breakfast (whatever it is) and put it on a table. Then go back to the bedroom and let your gentle touch and the smell of freshly made coffee from the kitchen wake your partner up.

"If you can't do the little things right, you will never do the big things right."

- William H. McRaven

19. Leave the house to your loved one alone.

LEAVE THE HOUSE TO YOUR LOVED ONE ALONE FOR A WHILE

Take the kids to the park while they are on spring break and let your partner enjoy the house on their own terms.

20. Fix your loved one's favorite dish.

Why wait for your loved one's birthday or a special celebration to fix their favorite dish?

FIX HIM HIS FAVORITE DISH

Do it today, do it just because. It will have a much more powerful impact.

21. Make loving exceptions.

Love Booster MAKE LOVING EXCEPTIONS

Do all of you love mashed potato, but he hates it? Make mashed potato for you but make a small pot of roasted potato too, just for him.

22. Perform stealthy good deeds and ghostly acts of kindness.

Love Booster PERFORM STEALTHY GOOD DEEDS AND GHOSTLY ACTS OF KINDNESS

Fold your partner's clothes on the bed, or hang them in the closet, say nothing. When your partner showers, secretly lay out pajamas for them, still warm from the dryer.

Happiness is like jam.
You can't spread even a little
without getting some on yourself."

- Anonymous

23. Send a message in a ...pocket.

SEND A MESSAGE IN A ...POCKET

Hide a loving note in your spouse's clothes for tomorrow so they find it while at work.

24. Empty the dishwasher before leaving for work.

EMPTY THE DISHWASHER BEFORE LEAVING FOR WORK.

Depending from who's doing this kind of chore more often, you might want to pitch in and do it yourself. It's not a big deal and it'll take you just a few minutes or so. Still, it sends a powerful message of not taking your loved one for granted.

"In the sweetness of friendship
let there be laughter,
and sharing of pleasures.
For in the dew of little things
the heart finds its morning
and is refreshed."

- Khalil Gibran

25. Make romantic graffiti.

Love Booster MAKE ROMANTIC
GRAFFITI

Use lipstick or soap to write a love message on the bathroom mirror. (Just be sure you try it in advance and you know what it takes to clean the message off the mirror!)

26. Interrupt, irresistibly.

Love Booster INTERRUPT, IRRESISTIBLY

While your love is cooking, go up behind them, and slide your arms around their waist. If your partner is reading or writing emails, nuzzle your face into the side of their neck and tell them how much you love them.

27. Snuggle on the couch.

Sit close to each other on the couch, possibly under the blanket and warming each other's feet.

After you've put the kids to bed, prepare some popcorn and a warm blanket. Then invite your loved one to watch a TV show together.

28. Hold hands while walking together.

Hold hands, especially when you're with your kids (for the very same reason as mentioned in *love booster* #9).

"We forget the little things,
so it's no wonder
some of us screw up
the big things."

- Neil Cavuto

29. Hug your partner from behind next time they are brushing their teeth.

Love Booster · HUG YOUR PARTNER FROM BEHIND NEXT TIME THEY ARE BRUSHING THEIR TEETH

Use the next opportunity when your loved one is brushing their teeth (or for that matter is doing any other activity where they can't be looking around much), go up behind your partner and slide your arms around them and simply hug them. It's powerful because it's unexpected.

30. Let them catch you looking.

Love Booster · LET THEM CATCH YOU LOOKING

Catch your love's eye while they are reading the newspaper or are concentrating. When they look up and see you, smile and tell them how much you love them.

31. Be sense-ible.

When walking past your loved one, brush by them with a quick touch. This could be just a quick touch to the small of the back, shoulder or waist.

32. Do one of your partner's chores, and sweep them off their feet.

Taking over a chore usually done by your partner can be a happy surprise. Without them knowing, pick a chore that your partner routinely does and do it yourself, and without any expectations of thanks.

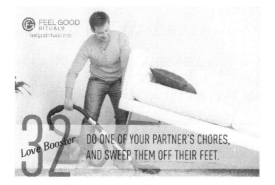

Love Booster 32 DO ONE OF YOUR PARTNER'S CHORES, AND SWEEP THEM OFF THEIR FEET.

If she usually does the vacuuming, why not do it yourself today? If he usually mows the lawn, why not mow it for him one weekend?

33. Place your arm around your loved one in public.

Love Booster 33 PLACE YOUR ARM AROUND YOUR LOVED ONE IN PUBLIC

34. Kiss your loved one on the cheek during commercials.

Do you find the commercials interrupting your favorite show annoying?

Love Booster 34 WHILE WATCHING TV TOGETHER, SOFTLY KISS YOUR LOVED ONE ON THE CHEEK DURING COMMERCIALS

Well, use that time and lean forward and softly kiss your loved one. No words needed. Chances are, your partner will close their eyes and smile because they can't help but feel good about what you just did!

35. For here, or to go? Pack a message for your lonely traveler.

Love Booster 35 FOR HERE, OR TO GO? PACK A MESSAGE FOR YOUR LONELY TRAVELER.

If your partner is going for a trip, put a note and a small present into their suitcase or laptop bag to be found later on the plane.

"When you are older you will understand how precious little things, seemingly of no value in themselves, can be loved and prized above all price when they convey the love and thoughtfulness of a good heart."

\- Edwin Booth

36. Rub your partner's neck while they're doing something.

Love Booster 36 RUB YOUR PARTNER'S NECK WHILE THEY'RE DOING SOMETHING

While your loved one is doing something, maybe writing an email or cooking dinner, just imagine how good it would feel to your loved one to feel your hands lovingly soothing their muscles around their neck? You don't have to be a professional masseur or a masseuse for your spouse to instantly feel more connected and loved.

37. Ask, "How was your day" ...and listen to the answer.

Ask your spouse about something they told you last time, and how that went.

That will show them you're listening. Listen carefully while not doing anything else.

38. Leave a message in (or on) your partner's car.

Write a "Missing you already!" note and stick it to the back of the sun visor so your partner can find it themselves. If you happen to live in an area where it gets cold, write a message on the car's frosty window "Kathy loves Mike". (If it doesn't get cold, write in the dust.)

"Kindness in words creates confidence. Kindness in thinking creates profoundness. Kindness in giving creates love."

- Lao Tzu

39. Invite your partner for lunch.

It doesn't have to be in a fancy restaurant; likely neither of you will have time for that. But it's a thoughtful and loving act, and a powerful message that says, "I'm thinking of you (even when you're busy.)"

40. Give your spouse a foot massage while watching television together.

A short foot massage every now and then can really help your spouse to relax, particularly after a long day of standing up and walking around. While you're watching television say nothing.

Just take your loved one's feet in your lap and start gently.

41. (For guys only) Be a gentleman. Open the car door for her!

Yes, it's an old fashioned custom and not seen much these days. That's another reason why you should be doing it!

It'll cost you just a couple of seconds but it'll send a tender message that you care.

42. Order something from a catalogue your spouse is looking at.

Pay attention to small wishes.

Listen when your partner makes a comment about something on television or in a catalogue. Go and buy that thing and show them you're listening.

43. Do something for your partner they hate doing.

We all hate doing certain things, right? So why don't you use that and do that thing for your loved ones every now and then (or constantly)? For example my wife hates paying bills, even online. What's the thing your partner hates doing?

"Everyone is trying to accomplish something big, not realizing that life is made up of little things."

- Frank A. Clark

44. Buy a little something - just because.

Small gestures say a lot. Buy your spouse a little something on your way home for no special reason —apart, from showing your thoughtfulness to the love of your life.

45. Get the kids to bed early, prepare some wine and cheese, and just talk.

It's a no fuss kind of meal and doesn't require much prep at all. You can enjoy over a movie, a good conversation, or a fun game together. And let's just be honest, a little wine always helps in the intimacy department."

46. Celebrate your own Valentine, any time.

Leave a candy where your precious one will find it with a note on saying "Thank you for being in my life."

47. Say "I love you" as many times you can. You really can't overdo it.

Finally, this is the most obvious one yet many times overlooked. Say "I love you" as many times you can. You can't overdo it.

"It's the little things that count, hundreds of 'em."

- Cliff Shaw

Make your loved one's day and surprise them even more!

Adding the element of surprise to your love note is always special to the receiver. No matter what mood you're in, it's always a delightful surprise to find a hidden love note somewhere.

For that reason, I prepared a special gift for you.

- GIFT: 25 more creative places to leave your love notes.

If you've already signed up for the bonus section of this book, then your permanent link to the bonus section and this cheat sheet is already waiting for you. If not, you can still do so by visiting:

http://geni.us/47bonuses

As mentioned earlier, in the bonus section you'll also find the 47 Little Love Boosters Golden Collection PDF, a one-pager with all the 47 Little Love Boosters at a glance, a success checklist and the audio book.

Last but not least, by activating your bonus section you'll be notified when a new release goes out or when I'm sending out goodies to my VIP readers.

CHAPTER 4

The Rewards

*"We will receive not
what we idly wish for
but what we justly earn.
Our rewards will always be
in exact proportion to our service."*

– Earl Nightingale

WHY IS DOING little things for each other so important?

Everyday Happiness

The most obvious reason is that you make your partner happy. Yes, it's that simple and that powerful. Because your spouse is special, make them feel that. That alone should be more than enough, right?

There's more.

There's another much more powerful element at play here.

Your Inner Voice

No matter how many books on improving your relationship you read, there will be times when you might explode, and start a nasty fight, despite what you may have learned.

Even when you totally mess up, forget to run that errand you promised, didn't call when you said you would, it won't matter as much, because you'll be in such a good place that those pesky annoyances won't seem so big.

Your loved one's inner voice becomes much more forgiving and understanding.

It prevents little annoyances from growing into more toxic behaviors such us blaming and criticism, to name just a few. These cause real damage to any relationship and leads to a prevailing negative perception of each other, silently deteriorating the whole relationship. That's why I call it the silent killer of relationships.

Because of the many positive interactions you've created with your partner, they are much more inclined to be understanding, forthcoming, and give you the benefit of the doubt.

This is because, *on a regular basis*, your partner is given proof that you think about them, that you care how they feel and genuinely want them to feel good.

If you think about it, this is why good friends are good friends. Good friends have had so many pleasant experiences together that when they argue over something or occasionally become offended by something the other might have said, it isn't reason enough to break up the friendship. They'll make up and remain good friends because they have invested in many positive experiences together. And you need to be friends before you can expect to be truly connected or achieve any kind of emotional intimacy.

Going out, doing fun things, or simply calling each other on the phone and discussing things, telling each other secrets, and doing small favors for one another; this is all stuff that good friends do. With all those little things, their ties grow stronger every day. This is what you want to achieve in your relationship.

The Best Insurance Policy You'll Ever Have

Making your *daily love deposits* to your love account acts like the best insurance policy you'll ever have.

It's your permanent cushion against the times when things in your relationship get bumpy.

Unlike many insurance policies, you can't pay in advance or at the end of the year. Instead, you must keep paying small amounts day by day, month by month, year after year, in order for this insurance policy to work.

Your Children

This is an aspect I can't emphasize enough and here's why.

Interestingly enough, when the struggle in our marriage was at its peak, it was our youngest son Nik, at the time aged four, who unknowingly pushed us in the right direction.

How?

One day the kindergarten teacher of our son invited us for a talk. It was a long sobering talk. The teacher told us that our son had been acting very aggressively. He seemed to enjoy hurting himself and at times he was dangerous to other children as well. As we sat there, listening to all the details, we got really scared. If you've seen the movie *We Need To Talk About Kevin* you know what I mean. It's a bit embarrassing to admit but it took us almost two years of visiting different child counselors and while trying to "fix" our son, we finally realized it was our relationship that needed to be fixed instead. That was our final wake up call.

This is another reminder and strong reason why it's vital to connect in meaningful ways with your partner every day, no matter how busy you are.

I believe the greatest gift that parents can give to their children is letting them experience firsthand their father cherishing their mother, and their mother adoring their father.

The greatest gift that parents can give to their children is to let them see how much their parents love each other.

Your children will be grateful to you, they just don't know it yet.

By seeing you being thoughtful and caring to your spouse (their dad or mom), subconsciously your children will form the very same positive behavior patterns they've learned from YOU and bring them into their own relationship later in their adult life.

What a great gift!

CHAPTER 5

Success Checklist

*"Remember that the happiest people
are not those getting more,
but those giving more."*

– H. Jackson Brown, Jr.

Forget Keeping Score and Lead the Way

The secret is what our grandparents already knew. It is in giving that we receive.

The love you give returns to you. It's also the only way you can generate any change for the better.

Yes, it's risky to invest yourself, especially if you've been disappointed a couple of times. But the past doesn't determine your future because your future hasn't been written yet. You're writing it right now.

It has been proven time and time again that couples who focus on the other's needs *without keeping score* are the ones who are successful and can enjoy the deep satisfaction that keeps their love growing even after many years of sharing their life together.

Therefore, start doing nice little things for your spouse even if currently it's only you who leads the way.

There is Nothing to be Embarrassed About

Especially if you're not used to doing nice little things for each other, or if you haven't been doing them for some time, you may feel a bit awkward about starting this.

Maybe you fear you'll be a little embarrassed? Maybe you worry your partner might ask you "what's wrong" or say, "This isn't like you."

That's awesome! They noticed! Don't say anything, or perhaps just say, "Nothing. I just remembered how much I love you."

Just remember this.

Nothing can be wrong with doing something nice for your loved one.

Never Expect Something in Return

While doing nice little things for our loved ones it gets easy to start counting and expecting something in return. Do it for your partner, do it because you'll make your spouse happy! Do it for your partner's smile and loving look. Do it even if your spouse doesn't notice. And even when they do, do something else again.

Do it just because.

Make it Easy to Remember

Especially at the beginning, it might be difficult for you to remember to ask yourself the most important question (you still remember what is it, don't you?).

Let's repeat the question. "What will I do for _____(fill in the name of your loved one) today?".

Of course you have to do something about it, but the first step is not to forget about it in the first place.

Here's a quick tip how you can make your life easier that worked well for me.

In order to avoid forgetting, you can set up a simple system that will gently remind you every day until you get used to it and it becomes part of your life style.

Simply set yourself a recurring alarm on your phone that goes off in the morning each day and asks you the most important question. I know, it doesn't sound particularly romantic (I mean the phone stuff), but it works.

Pay Attention

Notice what your spouse likes. This will give you new ideas how to make your spouse happy. Expand the list as time goes by.

Keep the list handy for when you need a quick peek, or want to amend it when you get an idea.

Here's a quick tip.

I keep a list of the little things my wife likes handy. For this I use my phone with a free note-taking application called Evernote. It works for me because it's always with me and I can easily add to the list. Sometimes I might get an idea and I'll email it to myself. But you can just use a piece of paper that you keep in your wallet just as well. The important thing is that you notice, remember and then act.

Persist

Have realistic expectations. In fact, you should expect that your partner might not notice or respond to your attempts at first. That's because your partner is simply not used to it.

Don't give up now. Continue softly and gently, knowing that there will come a point in time when your partner will start responding, but it may just take a while.

Don't worry, though. Your partner WILL notice.

Once your partner knows for sure that these acts of kindness are not a coincidence, you will see, feel and hear a positive reaction.

Then watch the magic start happening.

Summary

- Pick 10 ideas from the list and commit to doing something nice for your spouse every day for the next 10 days.
- Set yourself a recurring reminder that goes off each day for the next 10 days.
- Keep the list handy for a quick peep, or when you want to amend it. The best place is your phone, but a simple piece of paper in your wallet will work too.
- Notice what your spouse likes. This will give you new ideas. Combine them as you please and expand the list as time goes by. Make the list yours.
- Persist. Show your love by example and not by words alone.

Your Turn

Now you know how simple the *love boosters* really are. That's called awareness. But awareness alone is not enough—it's only half of success. You also need the other half, and that's action.

If you haven't done it already, make sure you have downloaded the Golden Collection PDF cheat sheet and the one-pager so you'll have inspiration whenever you're temporarily out of ideas. Furthermore, you might want to save the PDF to your phone so you can have a quick peek even when you don't have this book handy.

Or you might want to use the cheat sheet in the bonus section and amuse yourself by planting your love notes at places your loved one would have never imagined.

Whatever you do, the important thing is to start.

"It is the sweet, simple things of life which are the real ones after all."

- Laura Ingalls Wilder

Final Thoughts

IF YOU THINK about it, doing nice little things for each other is just common sense. Too often, though, it's common sense not being applied to common practice.

You CAN do a nice, little, sweet thing for your spouse even if that is just a simple "Thank you" and giving a loving look. You CAN give a little praise to your spouse and make them feel appreciated, even if that's just mentioning how beautifully the lawn was cut or how great your partner looks in that dress.

It's quite shocking to think that there will be people who have downloaded this book only to feel better about themselves, but who won't have even read this far! The fact that you're still here shows that you're an action taker. So don't let yourself down just before the finish line. Follow through with some immediate action, and persist.

Once you've finished this book, make a commitment to take immediate action. Commit to doing something nice for your spouse regularly, every day. Investing a couple of minutes a day to re-connect with your loved one is something you CAN stick with.

Even if you miss a day or two, you'll be fine. You might get sick or you'll be away for a while. That's okay as long as you don't forget. Be warned, though. After quick successes, you'll be tempted to back off a little. It's way too easy to resort to old habits of doing little or nothing for your relationship and expecting it'll take care of itself. You know it won't.

There is more good news. As you follow this book, you'll see the first positive signs of your efforts almost immediately. Still, with a little help from this book, the lasting positive effects will result from your consistent efforts. There's no way around that.

If necessary, use reminders, use your phone, stickers, notes... It might not sound particularly romantic to have to remind yourself to do something thoughtful for your spouse but you know what? Anything that'll make it easier for you to adopt a beautiful new love ritual of doing nice little things for your spouse will justify it. The rewards are great. The results are magical.

It might be a good idea to start writing a journal. If you haven't done it before, try it out. For the sake of the experience and the journey I encourage you to start now. Even though it's not necessary, I say this because you WILL reap huge benefits.

Journaling will help you get to know yourself and your partner much better. Through journaling, you will become more aware of the little things that your spouse likes and you like. The things you've done and the reaction you've received. You'll become a better partner. Furthermore, your journal will be a nice memory of your path toward the intimate marriage and relationship you desire and deserve.

Lastly, I hope you enjoyed this book as much as I enjoyed creating it for you.

If you're serious about making your relationship and your life the best it can be, if you want to enjoy a fulfilling relationship and you're looking for simple ways to ignite more passion, joy and excitement in your relationship starting right now, then I invite you to have a look at other books and publications of mine in the last section of this book or at:

http://www.feelgoodrituals.com.

About the Author

Marko Petkovic is the author of the Amazon Best-Sellers the *47 Little Love Boosters For A Happy Marriage*, the *Feel Good Marriage* and his latest book—*The 5 Little Love Rituals*. He is also the creator of feelgoodrituals.com, dedicated to helping people achieve healthy, fulfilling relationships, personal success, and abundance. He believes that successful relationships are acts of doing, not having, and can therefore be learned.

Married for more than fifteen years, Marko writes for couples who struggle balancing their professional work with home and raising kids while trying to be good partners to their life mates.

Marko believes seemingly overwhelming problems can and should be broken down into simple, actionable steps that anyone can start implementing immediately. In that spirit, he strives for all of his work to be practical and down-to-earth, teaching only things that work and pass the test of common sense.

Marko is also the father of two boys. He would like to consider himself to be a kickass husband and father, but he still screws up every now and then. When this happens, he says to himself, *"Tomorrow, I'll do better,"* and sees those everyday family challenges as inspiration for his own work. He starts his day early and believes that hope is not a plan.

Last Thing

THANK YOU for purchasing this book!

So, if you've landed here and read up to this point then the only thing left is to do me a small favor.

See, online bookstores use reviews to rank books AND many readers like you evaluate the quality of a title based solely on the feedback from others.

To put it simply :) Reviews are kind of a big deal to authors like me!

So, if you have a minute or so to write a couple of words about the book (good or bad!) today, that would be great! It would mean a world to me.

To leave your review, visit one of the links below:

Amazon: http://bit.ly/47reviewamazon

All other bookstores: http://bit.ly/47review

Not sure how to write a review?

Here's a simple template that you can use.

- What did you like most/least about the book?
- What's your most important takeaway or insight from the book?
- What did or will you start doing differently because of the book?
- What would you change about the book?
- Who would you recommend the book to the most?

It doesn't have to be lengthy or professional!

THANK YOU!

It means a great deal to me.

You May Also Love

The 5 Little Love Rituals
Connect and Keep Your Love Alive No Matter
How Busy You Are

Having read the *47 Little Love Boosters For a Happy Marriage* book, you now know that successful relationships **require lots of little, daily positive interactions.**

Therefore, if your goal is to maximize positive interactions with your partner, you have to find ways to **create bonding moments RIGHT NOW—** in the midst of the job and the kids and the bills and the colds...

When you get your copy of *The 5 Little Love Rituals book*, you will discover how to:

- Develop a habit of keeping up with each other's lives and so prevent ending up living with a stranger some day (page 53).
- Increase the level of physical intimacy between the two of you with no "sexpectations" and why this is one of the easiest (yet most connecting things) you can do. In the book I also share 18 simple ways how you can do that in a most natural way (page 71).
- Spend meaningful time together—even if your schedule is jam-packed and your days are exhausting. As a bonus you'll also get my free cheat sheet with 39 simple-to-implement ideas how you can juice up your relationship, even if you're a busy parent with young children (page 75).
- Provide mystery. We want to feel safe, but we also want to experience novelty. But how can you create mystery with the person you already know so well? Isn't getting to know someone well, by definition, the opposite of experiencing them as mysterious? On page 93 you'll learn 48 simple ways how you can keep creating a sense of adventure and novelty in your relationship even after many years of marriage or living together. This is not much talked about and yet peppering your relationship with some harmless thrill that you both enjoy is important for keeping

your love alive and to avoid getting bored with each other (like so many couples eventually do). You won't.

Available in eBook, Kindle and audio formats here:

http://bit.ly/5littleloverituals

Feel Good Marriage
7 Steps to a Rock Solid Relationship
Without Counseling

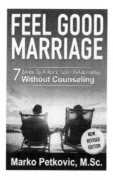

When you read this book you will:

- Understand not just why your partner does what they do, but why you yourself do what you do (and what to do about it).

- Learn the 10 fun facts about your unconscious and the surprising role it's playing in your relationship right now!
- Find the ONLY way to make your spouse change and the number one way to approach them if they won't.
- Discover the five magic questions to ask your partner so you'll always know what's really going on and the number one question you must stop asking your spouse if you want to know the truth.
- Learn what to do when you are criticized, even if you did nothing wrong, and how to disagree constructively while still standing your ground when emotions run hot.
- Make peace with the past and learn how to safely express your deepest needs, desires, and frustrations with heartfelt honesty without upsetting your partner.

... and a whole lot more!

Available here:

http://bit.ly/feelgoodmarriagebook

Get in Touch

If you'd like to get in touch with me please visit the link below.

Also, if you have an issue with accessing your bonus section, or you have some feedback, would like to work with me or simply chat, just pop me a message here:

http://geni.us/contactmarko

Disclaimer Notice

The author made his best effort to provide accurate and authoritative information. Even though the author of this material is well versed in the subject matter, the material contained in this book does not constitute professional advice. If professional assistance is required, the services of a competent professional should be sought.

All the material contained in this book is provided for educational and informational purposes only. No responsibility can be taken for any results or outcomes resulting from the use of this material.

While every attempt has been made to provide information that is both accurate and effective, the author does not assume any responsibility for the accuracy or use/misuse of this information.

Copyright

Made in the USA
Middletown, DE
22 September 2018